The Real Sherlock Holmes

The mysterious methods and curious history of a true mental specialist

Joe Riggs

Paperback ISBN 9781780922621
ePub ISBN 9781780922638
PDF ISBN 9781780922645

Published in the UK by MX Publishing
335 Princess Park Manor, Royal Drive, London, N11 3GX
www.mxpublishing.co.uk

Cover design by www.staunch.com

A Look Inside

Table of Contents

Down the rabbit hole we go.

"From the Astrologer came the Astronomer, from the Alchemist came the Chemist, from the Mesmerist came the Mental Specialist. The Charlatan is always the Pioneer. The Quack of Yesterday is the Professor of Tomorrow."

-Dr. Joseph Bell *(as portrayed by Ian Richardson)*

Dedicated to Elena:

The most beautiful and intelligent person I've ever known

Special Thanks To:

Mark Gatiss, a prolific writer in my opinion. A true hero for more reasons that I can name. Thank you so much for your work with the Undershaw Preservation Trust as well as the your incredible work in bringing Sherlock Holmes back to the forefront of the world's awareness.

Joe Riggs

Introduction

If you've made it this far into the book, that's more than most people ever do; and that is a factual statistic. For those of you who don't know me, my name is Joe Riggs. I am an internationally acclaimed Mentalist, Psychological Performer & Consultant. I have made appearances on innumerable radio and television spots. I have been repeatedly hailed as *"The Man Who Knows Too Much"* as well as *"The Real Sherlock Holmes."* The latter title is quite a heavy one, but then again; what I do often becomes very heavy.

Actually, the name "Sherlock Holmes" is an extremely important, even invaluable, one to me. However, we will delve into that soon enough. While what I do as a Mentalist is truly fascinating, to say the least; I feel it is my unusual background that sets me apart from other types of mental specialists.

I was raised by a professional psychic reader. Not only that, but I spent many of my childhood years in an exclusively metaphysical community. It was a place filled with all types of charlatans and linguistic swindlers. By the time I was fourteen, I had already powerfully mastered the methods of the psychic readers. From the tarot, to palmistry, to astrology and clairvoyance; I could execute and display them all, with one minor catch. I didn't believe any of it.

In fact, the majority of 'professional' psychic readers don't either, but we'll rarely catch them saying that. They know exactly how to do what they do; linguistically weaving together circular logic, elementary deductions, and self-fulfilling prophecies. They do so while maintaining the theatrics of a more spiritual methodology that naturally includes the use of their various toys and props.

Back to Sherlock Holmes: I can say with positivity that it was my very early obsession with Sir Arthur Conan Doyle's fictional consulting detective which kept me grounded and logical amidst the fantastical world of psychics and metaphysical charlatanry. Holmes' method of deductive reasoning and advanced observation seemed to come very naturally to me. I quickly incorporated the more advanced reading methods of the psychics with my newfound deductive and observational skills. My aptitude for these two very different 'mental' approaches led to my lifelong study of the human condition. Learning about psychology and the power of the mind led me to a mastery of skills that include: body language reading, Neuro Linguistic Programming (NLP), instant induction hypnosis, psychological and criminal profiling, and social engineering. The Fort Worth Star Telegram may have called me *"The Man Who Knows Too Much"* for a reason.

In this book, I am going to take you on an exciting, informative, and entertaining journey into the worlds of the psychic as well as the Mentalist. I am going to show you many of the key methods of the psychic readers, so you can know what to look out for. Not only that, but I am also going to delve into the world of the mental specialist or Mentalist, teaching you techniques and systems that empower you to do amazing things with your mind alone. If you choose to mix the two worlds together, that is up to you. I never had a choice. ~ Joe Riggs

Part I - Psychic Lies

We have all seen them. Most all of us have visited them: psychic readers, metaphysical shops, spiritual consultants, and if you're really serious; you may have even made the pilgrimage to Sedona. Whether you have or have not been taken in by this multi-million dollar industry whose primary products are circular logic, false hope, linguistic dances and cunning deception; it makes no difference. It is time to learn the methods of these charlatans so you can protect yourself against their ruses and dodges; not to discount the fun you will have with these skills at your disposal. I will let you and your imagination figure out what to do with them. I am here to teach you the skills, techniques and deceptions that are used every day, everywhere, on unsuspecting victims.

Psychics don't rely on tips from the 'spiritual realm' to warn them of impending disasters. Psychics don't predict their own deaths or diseases. They go to the dentist like the rest of us. They're as surprised and disturbed as the rest of us when they have to call a plumber or an electrician to fix some defect at home. Their planes are delayed without their being able to anticipate the delays. If they want to know something about Abraham Lincoln, they go to the library; they don't try to talk to Abe's spirit. In short, psychics live by the known laws of nature, except when they're playing their psychic games with people. Psychics aren't overly worried about other psychics reading their minds and revealing their innermost secrets to the world, and no casino has ever banned psychics from the gaming room. Why? Simply put: there is no need.

Summary of the topics covered in this section:

The Scam: This will blow your mind! Learn the terrifying secret behind 'The Scam' that psychics use to dupe every single person ('mark') with an unbelievably overt phrase that mocks the very participant!

Cold Reading: Cold reading is a series of generalizing and rephrasing techniques used by psychics, fortune-tellers, and the like, to determine or express details about another person.

Hot Reading: Hot reading is the gathering and use of foreknowledge about the client by the psychic reader.

Forer/Barnum Effect: "The Forer Effect" is also called "The Barnum Effect" after P.T. Barnum's astute observation that "we've got something for everyone." He noticed that, statistically, individuals will give high accuracy ratings to descriptions of their personality that supposedly are tailored specifically for them

Psychics Gone Wrong: Here, I describe how most psychics attempt to weave their way out of mistakes.

The Scam

You may feel slightly insulted by the end of this page, but do read on.

From as early as I can remember, I was being taught the 'seven areas of significance.' The psychics all knew these seven areas. I know that many psychic readers are taught as early as I was; however, some of them learn these categories are spiritually significant and may not even be aware of how they use their own methods.

The seven areas of importance are:

TRAVEL

HEALTH

EDUCATION

SEX

CAREER

AMBITIONS

MONEY

That's it. Seven words yet they cover every single question or topic a subject will ever have on their mind when they consult the psychic reader. A skilled reader will employ all the methods outlined in this section of the book whilst working within the framework of the seven aforementioned categories. This is a recipe for extremely powerful psychic readings. Yet, there is a twist, and a terrible twist at that.

How would you remember those seven words if your life depended on it? Psychics' lives technically do.

It is actually incredibly easy, and rather disturbing. We were taught to take the first letter of every word and remember the phrase: "T.H.E. S.C.A.M."

It's amazing how the phrase 'The Scam' is the very way to remember the scam, itself. As soon as I truly understood it, I quickly grew to find its implications disconcerting. Recently, Luke Jermay, a British Mentalist, taught this secret in one of his contributions to the Mentalism community. I was rather happy to see this old ruse being exposed. However, psychics conveniently forget their methods as these skills become second nature.

The next time you think about visiting a psychic, make sure you remember The Scam.

Cold Reading

"The currently-popular 'psychics' like Sylvia Browne, James Van Praagh, and John Edward, who are getting so much TV space on Montel Williams, Larry King, and other shows, employ a technique known as "cold reading." They tell the subjects nothing, but make guesses, put out suggestions, and ask questions. This is a very deceptive art, and the unwary observer may come away believing that unknown data was developed by some wondrous means. Not so." – James Randi

Cold Reading is an elegantly deceptive tool and is employed by some of the greatest 'mediums' of our time. Yet, this method is not exclusive to the television clairvoyant. Cold reading is used in just about every single psychic art form. From tarot reading to palmistry, cold reading is by far the most widely used and relied upon technique. I was exposed to masterful cold readers from as early as I can remember.

A little bit about you...

People close to you have been taking advantage of you. Your basic honesty has been getting in your way. Many opportunities that you have had offered to you in the past have had to be surrendered because you refuse to take advantage of others. You like to read books and articles to improve your mind. In fact, if you're not already in some sort of personal service business, you should be. You have an infinite capacity for understanding people's problems and you can sympathize with them. But you are firm when confronted with obstinacy or outright stupidity. Law

enforcement would be another field you understand. Your sense of justice is quite strong.

Was I right? Well, actually that was from astrologer Sydney Omar and it is a very old excerpt. A well delivered cold reading can be devastating in the right hands. This above example has nothing specific about it and yet it still has the power to hook just about anyone. Horoscopes captivate millions with vague statements, daily. Most psychics aren't that generic though; the above was written for a column intended for a mass audience. The experienced reader can learn a wealth of information from your appearance and body language before you've even begun. Reading people is an art form, in and of itself; yet even the most basic of 'people reading' techniques woven into a well-crafted cold reading can quickly turn into a psychic's gold mine.

Before starting the actual reading, the reader will typically try to elicit cooperation from you, by saying something such as, "I often see images that are a bit unclear and which may sometimes mean more to you than to me; if you help, we can together uncover new things about you." One of the most crucial elements of a convincing cold reading is that subjects are eager to make connections or reinterpret vague statements in any way that will help the reader appear to make specific predictions or intuitions about them. While the reader will do most of the talking, it is the subject who provides the meaning. We all fall for this.

The television mediums actually have it easiest. Their audience is already rapt before they arrive; not to mention that when a psychic performer works with a large group they can "Shotgun" their way to success. "Shotgunning" is a commonly used cold reading technique. The reader slowly offers a large quantity of very general information to an entire audience (some of which is very likely to be correct, near correct, or at the very least, provocative or evocative to someone present), then observes the audiences' reactions (especially their body language), and then narrows the scope; acknowledging particular people or concepts and refining their original statements according to specific people's reactions, targeting those with whom they have elicited the most emotional responses.

This technique is named after a shotgun, as it fires a cluster of small projectiles in the hope that one or more of the shots will strike the target. A majority of people in a room will, at some point for example, have lost an older relative or known at least one person with a common name like "Mike" or "John".

As I stated earlier, many readers learn these techniques without actually being aware of it. Former New Age practitioner Karla McLaren said, "I didn't understand that I had long used a form of cold reading in my own work! I was never taught cold reading and I never intended to defraud anyone; I simply picked up the technique through cultural osmosis." Sadly, this is the case, all too often. That is why, as potential marks for these charlatans; we must all educate ourselves and be alert and vigilant to amassing the 'right' type of knowledge with which to protect against these deceptive 'mystics.' The only thing that can save you from cons and charlatans is information. They spend enough time deceiving themselves; it's time we leave them to it.

Hot Reading

Hot reading is the procuring and use of foreknowledge when giving a psychic reading or demonstration. The reader can gain information about the person receiving the reading through a variety of means, such as background research or overhearing a conversation. Hot reading is commonly used in conjunction with cold reading (where no foreknowledge is available) and can explain how a psychic reader can get an extremely specific "hit" of accurate information.

The psychics may have clients schedule their appearance ahead of time, and then collect information using collaborators who pose as religious missionaries, magazine sales people, or similar roles. Such visitors can gain a wide understanding of a person from examining their home. The "psychic" may then be briefed on the information, and told where the person will sit in the audience.

A 2001 *Time* article reported that psychic John Edward allegedly utilized hot reading on an episode of his television show, *Crossing Over*, in which an audience member who received a reading was suspicious of prior behavior from Edward's aides. These aides had apparently struck up conversations with audience members and asked them to fill out cards detailing their family trees before the show. In December 2001, Edward was alleged to have used foreknowledge to 'hot read' in an episode of the television show *Dateline*. The show depicted a 'reading' Edward did for a cameraman that was based on knowledge gained in conversation between the two, hours previously. Edward presented his dramatic 'reading' as if he was unaware of the cameraman's background. In his 2001 book, John Edward denied ever using foreknowledge, or any types of cold or hot readings. Clearly, he would never do such a thing!

In one of the live shows of *Beyond*, James Van Praagh was observed signing books and chatting with a woman he learned was from Italy. During the taping, he asked that same section if there was "someone from another country". To the television audience, this would have looked incredible when she raised her hand. He had used the hot reading technique of gaining foreknowledge. This is all absolutely true. This is happening every day. In the cyber age, is it really all that hard for a professional medium to find out about you? Facebook and Twitter are surely the new addiction of the investigative charlatan...

Forer/Barnum Effect

The Forer Effect relies in part on the eagerness of people to fill in details and make connections between what is said and some aspect of their own lives; often searching their entire life's history to find some connection, or reinterpreting general statements in a number of different possible ways, so as to make them apply to themselves.

"Barnum Statements" (named after P.T. Barnum, the American showman) are statements that seem personal, yet apply to many people. While seemingly specific, such statements are often open-ended or give the reader the maximum amount of "wiggle room" to generalize as necessary in a reading. They are designed to elicit identifying responses from people. The statements can then be woven into longer and more sophisticated paragraphs and seem to reveal great amounts of detail about a person. A talented and charismatic reader can sometimes even force a subject into admitting a connection by demanding, over and over, that they acknowledge a particular statement as having some relevance and maintaining that they just aren't thinking hard enough, or are repressing some important memory.

Common Barnum Statements that display the Forer Effect:

"I sense that you are sometimes insecure, especially with people you don't know very well."

"You have a box of old unsorted photographs in your house."

"You had an accident when you were a child involving water."

"You're having problems with a friend or relative."

"Your father passed on due to problems in his chest or abdomen."

Regarding the last statement, if the subject is old enough, his or her father is quite likely to have died, and this statement would easily apply to a number of conditions such as heart disease, pneumonia, diabetes, most forms of cancer, and in fact to a great majority of causes of death.

Barnum Statements in the hands of someone who is already adept at reading people can take a medium or psychic reader to the heights of fame. I would say this applies to, most likely…every famous psychic you've ever seen, heard of, or read.

Psychics Gone Wrong

This is, indeed, my favorite section of Part I for innumerable reasons, and it is also the least clever department in the psychic reading field. First of all, the clients are generally predisposed to 'metaphysical' things, or at least believe in the psychics' or mediums' abilities to some extent. Therefore, the cards are always stacked in the favor of the psychic reader, because the client already wants to believe.

Nearly all psychics, including James van Praagh and John Edward, repeatedly warn their marks that they aren't always accurate, that they don't know how their power works, and that they occasionally misinterpret things; but they never give any sign that they are not really communicating with the dead.

Psychics also have to stack the deck so as to convince the mark that he or she will be the reason for success or failure. This is actually true because it is the subject that will provide all the vital information that seems so shocking and revealing. It is human nature to innately search for patterns and meaning, so this is not a difficult feat. The subject will bring significance to much of what the reader may throw at him or her. If they bring up "June" and get no response, they make the mark feel like they're not remembering properly. If they say "8, the 8th month, 8-years, August" and somebody bites by saying, "Dad died in August," the subject now thinks it was the psychic who told her that fact rather than the other way around. They will say things like "I see a watch, a bracelet, something on the wrist" and the subject says "I put my necklace in mom's casket." They then say "Right. She thanks you for it, too." Everybody perceives they knew she put a necklace in the casket and they will forget that the reader was originally verbally fishing for some jewelry on the wrist.

If the reader encounters a skeptical subject or an irretrievable miss they will almost always default to, "you're blocking the energy, try to open up, clear you mind," or some variation upon that theme. It is never the fault of the psychic, ever. What a perfect profession to be in, and often lucrative. Preying on people's emotions and grief is far from my style and I hope that you have learned some invaluable tools.

Alright, now we're off to Part II:

Mental Spies

It's time to learn some wonderfully mental things…

Part II - Mental Spies

It's time to take an inside look at some of the tools I use as a Mentalist that can expand your mind-power, super charge your memory, heighten your deductive and observational powers, and transform the way you think. After being raised by the psychics, mastering their methods and realizing that I wasn't interested in that lifestyle, I had to figure out what to do with my unusual skillset. Mentalism seemed to be the perfect field upon which the integration of my preexisting skills would be the most useful.

My lifelong obsession with Sherlock Holmes & deduction really started to really flourish and show itself once I dove into the psychological arts. I've spent the rest of my life studying: Human Behavior, Body Language Reading, Neuro Linguistic Programming, Psychological Profiling, Verbal & Nonverbal Suggestion, various forms of Rapid and Instant Induction

Hypnosis, Deductive Investigation, Observational Analysis, Deception & Lie Detection, and the list goes on.

All of these areas of study have resulted in my being hailed by the media as *"The Man Who Knows Too Much"* and *'The Real Sherlock Holmes."* In mere seconds, and often before introduction are made, I can ascertain a wealth of knowledge about a person much like my beloved mentor Sherlock Holmes.

While it would be literally impossible to take you from where you are, to where I am in one book, I can give you some extremely powerful tools and techniques that will get you started on your journey to mental master. I have handpicked some of the core methods that I and droves of other mental specialists employ regularly.

Summary of the topics covered in this section:

Feeding the Brain | How what you eat and drink dramatically affects your brain power - make the changes

Strengthening the Mind | Tips, tricks, riddles & ruses to sharpen your mental faculty

Memory 101 | Advance your memory: what you need to know

Memorizing Massive Numbers | Learn to be a walking computer - master this simple system

The Memory Palace (Modi) | All the great Mind Masters use it. Did you know Sherlock Holmes used it?

Deduction & Observation | Using your deductive and observational powers to their fullest potentials

Body Language | Learning the most valuable cues and signs to spot deceptions and untold intentions

The NLP Breakdown | Neuro Linguistic Programming – Mind Control, influence & persuasion

Feed Your Brain

"Your memory, attention span, and ability to learn benefit from your choice of foods." -Cynthia Green, PhD, Founder and Director of the Memory Enhancement Program at Mount Sinai School of Medicine in New York City

1. **Avoid sugar.** Any simple carbohydrates can give you "brain fog." Sometimes called the "sugar blues," this sluggish feeling makes it hard to think clearly. It results from the insulin rushing into the bloodstream to counteract the sugar rush. Avoid pasta, sugars, white bread and potato chips before any important mental tasks.

2. **Seafood.** Seafood like salmon, albacore tuna, mackerel, and sardines are packed with Omega-3 fatty acids, and other powerful and versatile nutrients that are essential for a healthy mind. About 40% of the fatty acids in brain cell membranes are DHA, one of the main Omega-3 fatty acids in fish oil. Experts believe it's probably necessary for transmitting signals between brain cells.

3. **Leafy Greens and Cruciferous Veggies.** Pile your plate high with salads, stir-fries, and side dishes with broccoli, cauliflower, cabbage, kale, Bok Choy, and Brussels sprouts. They're filled with antioxidants like vitamin C and plant compounds called Carotenoids, which are particularly powerful protectors of your precious brain.

4. **Avocado, Oils, Nuts, and Seeds.** They all contain another important antioxidant: vitamin E. In one study,

researchers found that people who consumed moderate amounts vitamin E—from food, not supplements—lowered their risk of AD by 67%.

5. **Chocolate**. Sweeten your brain-boosting diet with the dark kind (at least 70% cocoa); it contains flavonoids, another class of antioxidants that some research links to brain health. Other flavonoid-rich foods include apples, red and purple grapes, red wine, onions, tea, and beer.

6. **Berries**. Research indicates these antioxidant powerhouses may protect your brain, although the mechanism isn't fully understood. Some scientists think they help to build healthy connections between brain cells.

7. **Whole grains**. Fiber-rich oatmeal, oat bran, and brown rice stabilize blood glucose (sugar) levels, compared with refined carbs like white bread and sugary foods. Your body digests these simple sugars quickly, so you have a sudden energy spike—and subsequent plummet.

8. **Water**. Every cell in your body needs water to thrive, and your brain cells are no exception; in fact, about three-quarters of your brain is water. A small Ohio University study found that people whose bodies were well hydrated scored significantly better on tests of brainpower, compared with those who weren't drinking enough.

9. **Coffee**. Caffeine is another substance wherein the dose makes the poison: In excess, it can cause brain fog, but in moderate amounts, caffeine can improve attention span, reaction time, and other brain skills. A 2007 French study found that women over 65 who drank three or more cups of coffee a day were better able to recall words than women who consumed little or none. Another review showed that coffee drinkers may cut AD risk by up to 30%.

10. **Alcohol (in moderation)**. While chronic, heavy drinking can cause serious dementia, research shows that indulging lightly seems to protect the brain. Small amounts of alcohol may protect both the heart and brain by preventing blockages in blood vessels. This is not a license to party, I promise.

Strengthening Your Mind

1. **Breathe deeply.** More air in means more oxygen in your blood, and therefore in your brain. Breathe through your nose and you'll notice that you use your diaphragm more, drawing air deeper into your lungs. Several deep breaths can also help to relax you, which is conducive to clearer thinking.

2. **Exercise.** Long term exercise can boost brainpower, which isn't surprising. Anything that affects physical health in a positive way probably helps the brain, too. Recent research, though, shows that cognitive function is improved immediately after just ten minutes of aerobic exercise. If you need a brain recharge, you might want to walk up and down the stairs a few times.

3. **Mindfulness exercises.** Concentration and clear thinking are more or less automatic once you remove distractions. Learn to stop and watch your busy mind. As you notice things that are subtly bothering you, deal with them. This might mean making a phone call you need to make, or putting things on a list so you can forget them for now. With practice, this becomes easier; and your thinking becomes more powerful. Puzzles, Crosswords & Cyphers are wonderful tools. See Appendix.

4. **Use dead time.** This is time that is otherwise wasted or just under-utilized. Driving time, time spent in waiting rooms, or even time spent mowing your yard can be included in this. With a iPod or Mp3 player, you can start to use this time to listen to audio books. You may spend 200 hours a year in your car. What could you learn in that time?

5. **Speed reading**. Contrary to what many believe, your comprehension of material often goes up when you learn to speed-read. You get to learn a lot more in less time. Anyone can do it, and it is an infinitely great brain exercise.

6. **Phosphotidyl Serine** (**PS**). This supplement has been shown in clinical studies to increase lucidity and rate of learning. It activates cell-to-cell communication, helps regulate cell growth, improves the functioning of the special receptors found on cells, and prepares cells for activity. In other words, it can help your brain power. It's also thought to reverse memory decline. Phosphotidyl Serine has no known adverse side effects.

7. **Vinpocetine**. This extract, derived from an alkaloid found in the Periwinkle plant, is used as a Cerebral Vasodilator. It increases blood flow to the brain, which improves its oxygenation and thereby increases mental alertness and acuity. Research suggests it may also be the most powerful memory enhancer available to date.

8. **Gingko Biloba**. The leaves of this tree have been proven to increase blood flow to the brain. The trees are often planted in parks, and if you like; you can chew a few for a brain boost. However, it is also inexpensive to buy the capsules or tea at any health food store.

9. **Study/Listen to Classical Music**. In a study at the University of California, researchers found that children who studied piano, were much better at solving puzzles, and when tested, scored 80% higher in spatial intelligence than the non-musical group. I am an avid musician myself; I play over 7 stringed instruments. Let's not forget Sherlock Holmes is written as an extraordinary violinist.

10. **Imaginary friends**. This is not a joke! This has been used by some of the top experts in the field, including

myself. Talking to, and getting advice from, characters in your mind can be a great way to access the information in your subconscious, which is a part of the brain to which we rarely have access. Imagine a conversation with a person who has a lot of knowledge into the area in which you want advice. Seriously, you will amaze yourself.

Memory 101

"Memory is the treasury and guardian of all things." -
Marcus Tullius Cicero

In the past, many experts were fond of describing memory as a sort of tiny filing cabinet full of individual memory folders in which information is stored away. Others likened memory to a neural supercomputer wedged under the human scalp. But today, experts believe that memory is far more complex and elusive than that; and that it is located not in one particular place in the brain, but is instead a brain-wide process.

They say that, "you can't teach an old dog, new tricks" but when it comes to the brain, scientists have discovered that this old adage simply isn't true. The human brain has an astonishing ability to adapt and change, even into old age. This ability is known as neuroplasticity. With the right stimulation, your brain can form new neural pathways, alter existing connections, and adapt and react in ever-changing ways.

The brain's incredible ability to reshape itself holds true when it comes to learning and memory. You can harness the natural power of neuroplasticity to increase your cognitive abilities, enhance your ability to learn new information, and improve your memory. The best part is that it's not nearly as complex or difficult as it may seem.

By the end of the next few pages you will be able to do things you've never been able to do before. If you follow along you will be learning some of the most powerful mental techniques in use today. By the end of this book you will have already learned a massive amount of information that I can't even mention yet. You would close this book in pure doubt. But what I am saying is not only true, it's surefire. It is time for you to leap down the rabbit hole.

You are about to amaze yourself while unlocking the unlimited hidden potential of your own mind...

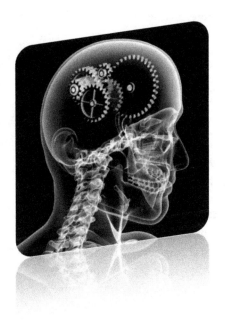

Memorizing Massive Numbers

Numbers, or digit strings, are considered by many mnemonists and cognitive scientists to be the most difficult data to memorize. If they are both so abstract and difficult, how did Hideaki Tomoyori of Japan memorize "π" which most of us know to mean approximately 3.14, to more than 10,000 specific decimal digits further than that? The answer is phonetic encoding, or translation of the abstract to the concrete. Hideaki used what I'm teaching you, here. Just learn these NINE pieces of information, and get ready!

The average person can only hold seven or fewer numbers in their working memory at any given time, using vocal repetition as an aid. Using phonetic encoding, trained subjects can memorize all of the area codes in the United States within a 24-hour period. By encoding abstract data first as letters, then as nouns, one can accurately store and recall hundreds of items (images) both forwards and backwards.

This introduction to phonetic encoding will provide an overview of the consonant system mnemonic, which encodes numbers as consonants of the English language. In this system of encoding, neither vowels ("a, e, i, o, u"), nor the letters "w," "h," or "y" have any numerical value. Numbers are converted into consonants, which are then associated with nouns and images that you create. Hang in there, Friends, the examples make this method simple to learn and use.

Here are the encoding pairs that Tomoyori used to recall 10,000 numbers without error. Numbers are encoded as indicated below, and suggestions for remembering the pairings are provided in parentheses:

1. t or d (both like 1, have a single downstroke)
2. n (two downstrokes)
3. m (three downstrokes)
4. r (the last letter of "four" is "r")
5. L (you have five fingers on your Left hand)
6. j, ch, soft g, sh ("J" is a near mirror-image of "6") (Ex: Jelly, CHips, garaGe, SHoe)
7. k, hard g, hard c ("7" side-by-side with a mirror image form a sideways "K") (Ex: Kite, Goat, Cat)
8. f, v, ph ("8" is similar to the lower-case cursive "f") (Ex: Flame, Vest, graPH)
9. p or b (9 is a mirror-image of "P")
0. z, s, soft c (0 signifies "zero") (Ex: Zipper, Scarf, iCe)

Using the above conversion table, 8209 could equal "fan" (82) and "soap" (09), thus a 'fan made of soap.' Numbers are converted to words by the phonetics (sounds), and spelling is unimportant. Thus: 8762 = FKSHN = fikshun = fiction (vowels possess no value). Use whichever vowels you want. If you can then place one such composite image at 20 preselected locations (**loci**), you will memorize 80 numbers with ease. You will learn to do this with ease in the '**Memory Palace**' section.

Likewise, repeated letters are represented by a single number unless two separate sounds are made: 3230 = MNMS = Minnie Mouse ("nn" represents the single 2)

Encoding, and improved abstract recall, can be used to learn 500 foreign vocabulary words in a single 12-hour session or memorize all of the ticker symbols on the New York Stock Exchange! Increase your recall capacity by 500% and you can literally quintuple your lifetime learning capacity. Learn to efficiently encode the abstract and the results can and are, almost superhuman. You may want to start by converting phone numbers into words and then images. Where to store them comes next...

The Memory Palace (Method of Loci)

"I consider that a man's brain originally is like a little empty attic, and you have to stock it with such furniture as you choose. A fool takes in all the lumber of every sort that he comes across, so that the knowledge which might be useful to him gets crowded out, or at best is jumbled up with a lot of other things, so that he has a difficulty in laying his hands upon it." —Sherlock Holmes in 'A Study in Scarlet.'

That's right. Arthur Conan Doyle was on the right track when he attributed his fictional consulting detective's 'mental powers' to be the result of a well-organized 'memory attic' system. While the 'Memory Palace' system that is widely employed today isn't necessarily associated with Sherlock Holmes, I believe the above quote should be given the credit it deserves. Now, let's get on to what the Memory Palace (or Method of Loci) actually is. This is going to get historically deep for a moment, but then we will break it down so you can create yours, NOW!

The Method of Loci ("loci" is the plural form of the Latin word "locus," meaning "place" or "location"), also called the Memory Palace, is a mnemonic device introduced in ancient Roman rhetorical treatises (as described in the anonymous *Rhetorica ad Herennium*, Cicero's *De Oratore*, and Quintilian's *Institutio Oratoria*). It relies on memorized spatial relationships to establish order and recollect memorial content. The term is most often found in specialized works on psychology, neurobiology and memory; though it was used in the same general way at least as early as the first half of the nineteenth century in works on rhetoric, logic and philosophy.

The Method of Loci is also commonly called the "mental walk." In basic terms, it is a method of memory enhancement which uses visualization to organize and recall information. Many memory contest champions claim to use this technique in order to recall faces, digits, and lists of words. These champions' successes have little to do with brain structure or intelligence, but more to do with their technique of using regions of their brain that have to do with spatial learning. Those parts of the brain that contribute most significantly to this technique include the Medial Parietal Cortex, Retrosplenial Cortex, and the right posterior Hippocampus.

In other words, the ability to do this does not lie in preexisting intelligence, but rather it is a learned tool.

CREATING YOUR MEMORY PALACE

The whole memory palace technique is based on the fact that we're extremely good at remembering places we know. So, the first step is to create a memory palace of your choosing in your mind's eye. A memory palace is essentially a physical location that you are very familiar with such as your home, or route to work; it can be any place you know well as long as you can clearly visualize each room or landmark within your memory palace with little to no effort. Everyone has a place they can choose. It is entirely up to you, choose your first 'memory palace' and map it out well in your mind. Really visualize this place, take the route, walk through the house, and your palace will be established.

DEFINING YOUR ROUTE

The second step is to trace a clearly defined route through your memory palace and visualize particular objects along the way. If you are considering your home for example, your route may start with your front door. You may enter into a hallway and notice a mirror hanging on the wall. Start with one object per room and

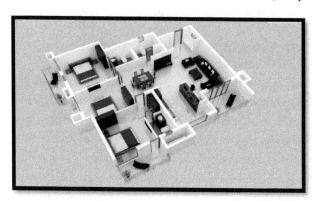

follow an easy path (such as, left to right) until you are back at your starting point.

Practice following this route in your memory palace, making an effort to remember each specific object in order. This shouldn't be hard to do if you choose a place deeply embedded within your mind; consider the house you grew up in. Each object you see and encounter is known as a 'memory peg'. Start with one object or 'memory peg' for every room in your palace, or every stop on your route. A simple example would be: you walk through the front door and see the coat rack, then you walk into the kitchen and notice the stove, then you walk into the garage and notice the ladder. Coat rack (front door), stove (kitchen), and ladder (garage): already, you have three 'memory pegs' in three different rooms in your Memory Palace.

USING YOUR MEMORY PEGS

Now think of something that you'd like to remember, such as a shopping list or your agenda for the week ahead. Place items in a particular order and integrate each with a memory peg (object) within your memory palace. It helps to conceptualize objects as being bizarre or perhaps cartoon-like at this stage. Memory does, after all, perform best when operating in a strong, visual way.

Since we created three pegs in the above example, the coat rack, the stove and the ladder; we can now utilize those pegs. If your grocery list only consisted of three items such as milk, bread and cheese you would then 'peg' them one at a time. Your first peg in the example is the coatrack; you walk through the front door and see the coatrack. So all you have to do is visually connect 'milk' and 'coatrack.' It is important to make your images as animated and bizarre as possible, so see the coatrack spewing milk from all its ends. At this point you would take a moment to really 'see' this image, and burn it into your mind. Now you would connect 'bread' to 'stove.' Keeping in mind that merely getting bread out of a stove isn't dramatic enough for memory. So I would see a man beating the stove to pieces with a gigantic loaf of bread. Done and done. Now just connect 'cheese' to 'ladder' i.e. A man is trying to climb the ladder and failing because it's made of cheese.

Your simple list would now be committed to memory. At the store, all you ever need to do is walk through your mental memory palace and your grocery list will fly right back at you. You will walk through the door and see milk spewing from the coatrack, then you would walk into the kitchen only to find a man beating the stove with a ridiculous loaf of bread, you then walk into the garage and see a man climbing the cheese ladder. "Milk, bread and cheese" is a pretty easy list to remember without a palace, yet you can see the power of the method.

The amazing thing is that your memory palace is EVERY bit as effective at storing enormous amounts of information as it is storing very small bits. Now that you have your own memory palace, expand it. From one peg in each room, upgrade to five or ten pegs in each room. In time, many of you will add additional rooms and wings. To set multiple pegs in each room, it is always best to close your eyes and see yourself inside that room. Then scan the room from left to right in your memory, and every single significant thing that you come across as you scan becomes a peg.

Start by creating five or ten pegs per room. Every time you mentally walk through the rooms in your memory palace you should be able to scan each room from left to right and spot all your predetermined memory pegs. In my palace, the living room is: couch, TV, printer, patio door and bookshelf. These are the five things that stand out the most when I mentally scan my living room from left to right. In recent years, I've gone back and expanded the list to have up to twenty pegs per room. It's your mind, it's your memory palace, and you get to make it; so create it the way you want it. Remember to start small at first, with no more than five or ten per room. Get good at utilizing and retrieving that much information before expanding it.

Your memory palace will serve you faithfully the rest of your life if you keep it fresh and active.

Test Your Skills

Time to test your skills: you are literally about to learn a list of twenty random words, forward and backward with little to no effort. Try this and you will amaze yourself. I do this with lists of

20-50 words often in demonstrations. You will need the first four rooms of your memory palace, with five pegs in each.

In total, you will need twenty pegs in your palace. If you placed five pegs per room, you'll only need the first four rooms. That will give you pegs for twenty items. You'll walk through those four rooms in a moment and construct the images, then later recall everything, both in and out of order! Remember to use BIZARRE images to attach the words to your pegs.

The List:

1.	Shoe	Attach this to Peg 1, Room 1.
2.	Bike	Attach this to Peg 2, Room 1.
3.	Remote	Attach this to Peg 3, Room 1.
4.	Cellphone	Attach this to Peg 4, Room 1.
5.	Shopping Cart	Attach this to Peg 5, Room 1.
6.	Knife	Attach this to Peg 1, Room 2.
7.	Hat	Attach this to Peg 2, Room 2.
8.	Horse	Attach this to Peg 3, Room 2.
9.	Skyscraper	Attach this to Peg 4, Room 2.
10.	Banana	Attach this to Peg 5, Room 2.
11.	Candle	Attach this to Peg 1, Room 3.
12.	Playing Cards	Attach this to Peg 2, Room 3.
13.	Briefcase	Attach this to Peg 3, Room 3.
14.	Sword	Attach this to Peg 4, Room 3.
15.	Laptop	Attach this to Peg 5, Room 3.
16.	Car	Attach this to Peg 1, Room 4.
17.	Boat	Attach this to Peg 2, Room 4.
18.	Scarf	Attach this to Peg 3, Room 4.
19.	Guitar	Attach this to Peg 4, Room 4.
20.	Scissors	Attach this to Peg 5, Room 4.

After you have created a bizarre and often animated mental image to connect each word to its corresponding peg in your memory palace, come back in fifteen minutes and see how many you can write down. Then come back in an hour and see how perfectly you still do. Lastly, consider everything you can do with this.

STORING LARGE NUMBERS

Earlier, I mentioned we would get back to storing large or massive numbers. Well, this is it. Using your memory palace and the phonetic encoding system from earlier, you can memorize incredible strings of numbers. You'll recall Hideaki Tomoyori of Japan who memorized π to more than 10,000 digits. This is how he did it:

1. Break down the number to be memorized, into a series of words using phonetic encoding.
2. Using your memory palace, attach each word, in order, to the pegs in each room of your palace.

Example:

Let us say that the number you want to remember is a serial number with ten digits: **1442749119**.

We can now break this down into pairs: **14, 42, 74, 91,** and **19**.

These are now ready to be converted into words; for instance: **Tire, Rain, Car, Boat & Tub**. (TiRe, RaiN, CaR, BoaT, TuB.)

Now we only have five **WORDS** to remember, rather than **TEN** digits.

Using only **ONE** room in your memory palace, you can now attach these five words to pegs using the mental imagery system we learned previously.

If your palace had ten rooms, with ten pegs in each room, you could learn a number one HUNDRED digits in length, in a few minutes. That looks like this:

8,767,534,321,238,765,978,056,423,123,457,689,543,761,232,386,754,127,645,08 9,707,689,124,268,079,523,187,452,097,845,128,967,452,389.

It may look slightly insane, but think about it: I have ten pegs per room in my memory palace. So that scary number is only fifty words and those fifty words take up only five rooms. Who doesn't have a memory palace with at least five rooms? I can just close my eyes, take a walk through my palace, and call out numbers as I go.

I've done it, and the more you use your memory palace combined with the phonetic encoding system, the easier they become and the more adept you become at using them. They become second nature.

Test Your Skills

Most of us will never have to memorize a number as large as the one above, but being able to recall very large numbers is a very useful and amazing skill. Here is an exercise to get you started:

Take a dollar out of your pocket. Analyze the serial number, and break it down into words. You can stick to the pattern of forming words out of 2 digit pairs, or you can create words out of 3 and 4 digit groupings. So long as the word's consonants decode back into the digits again. Take the word "mentalist" for example. Mentalist actually contains how many numbers? It has **SIX**! Six digits in one word! MeNTaLiST = 321501 or 321,501.

Break your serial number into however many words it takes, and then store those words in your palace.

See if you can recall them in an hour. Then start over with a fresh serial number. As you get better at this, you will notice it becomes almost automatic. Are you feeling any closer to omniscience? Keep reading.

Deduction & Observational Powers

"You see, but you do not observe. The distinction is clear." –
Sherlock Holmes

Stop Knowing and Notice

Much like Sherlock Holmes an adept Mentalist can gather a
wealth of information from a person or place within minutes, or
even seconds. Sherlock may be fictional, but his tools and powers
are not. Let's develop them.

Whenever you are faced with any new person, situation or
problem, you must first observe. Observation requires
detachment. Imagine one of those intense, icy glares from the
character of Sherlock Holmes as he would objectively scan a
room, taking in every detail. If you are emotionally involved, your
observation will be colored by your emotions.

You must become as detached as possible. Just allow what is there
to present itself to you. Open up your senses. Really listen, and let
the sounds impact you. Notice the smells. Look with the eyes of
an eagle: sharp, precise, and missing nothing. Be alert to every
movement, every clue, and anything that is out of the ordinary.

If you are emotionally reacting to a person or problem, you have
already lost objectivity, and pre-judged. You have narrowed your
mind by predefining your feelings. When you first start out, you
must be like a Taoist. You know nothing at this point. Sherlock
Holmes stressed not pre-judging a situation before the facts have
been observed and gathered.

"It is a capital mistake to theorize before one has data. Insensibly one begins to twist facts to suit theories, instead of theories to suit facts" – S.H.

Whilst we strive to be as objective as possible, the way a thing appears is always affected by the perspective from which we view it. To alleviate this obvious flaw, we must try and observe situations and problems from as many different angles and vantage points as possible.

True deduction and observation can only occur through a certain amount of self-annihilation! In other words, "you" have to shut up! You need to get yourself completely out of the way so that you can perceive clearly. As Krishnamurti said, "Learning is the very essence of humility." So get quiet. Get still. Look and see what is there.

So you've looked, you've listened, you've touched, tasted and smelled. You've gone in with your senses wide open and your mind quiet and alert. You've moved around both physically and mentally, taking up different positions, perceiving your situation or problem from different angles.

In looking, you are learning. When you see with fresh eyes, unclouded by what you think you know, your powers of deduction and observation become like that of a human computer. All systems are on alert. Your vision is sharper. There is no interference. The trance of listening to the incessant ramblings of your mind is finally broken. Suddenly, you find yourself in the moment, experiencing, and alive to all that is front of you.

"I see no more than you, but I have trained myself to notice what I see." –S.H.

This is a profoundly brain-enhancing state in which to be. In the state of silence and perceiving, you will be filled with what has been described as the 'mystical wind' of pure powerful intelligence.

Start seeing the world around you the way it is, instead of the way you 'feel' it to be. Observe.

Gathering the Facts

As you observe, you gather the facts. You are looking to see the components of the situation or problem. You soak up everything. You use the six question system (what, why, when, how, where, and who) to gather every ounce of information. You ask those questions of everything and everyone. You ask those questions aloud and with your senses: searching, seeking, questioning. Then, become totally receptive to the answers.

Putting the Pieces Together - Deduction

Think of a jigsaw puzzle. When you have all the pieces, and they are all in front of you, you can then start to analyze where they go and how they fit together. The more pieces you have, the easier it is to see what the big picture will be. So the more angles from which you have observed a problem, and the more facts you have gathered about it, the more able you become to see the final solution.

With the jigsaw, you might look for the pieces with straight edges, to get you started. You are looking for patterns that you can build on. Ask yourself if there are patterns in the problem that enable you to see its cause. Are there patterns in the person's behavior that enable you to see their true intentions? You take the pieces of the jigsaw, the facts, and you begin to think about how they fit together, how they relate to one another, how one links to the other and what effect that has on the overall picture.

"Each fact is suggestive in itself. Together they have a cumulative force." –S.H.

I can't hand you the answers. I can only give you the tools to perceive the answers for yourself. Follow these methods and you will, without fail, start to see every situation, problem and person in a very new way.

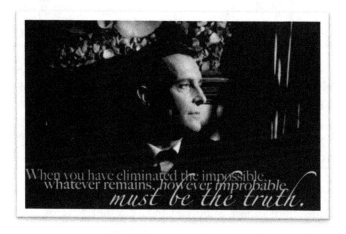

Body Language

A huge part of my work as a Mentalist is mastering the very delicate art of reading people's body language on the spot, and using it to gain invaluable information.

Body language refers to the nonverbal signals that we use to communicate. According to experts, these nonverbal signals make up a staggering part of daily communication. From our facial expressions to our body movements, the things we don't say are almost always more important than the things we do. Being able to speak this silent language is an amazing tool.

According to various researchers, body language is thought to account for between 50 to 70 percent of all communication. Understanding body language is important, but it is also essential to remember to note other cues such as context and to look at signals as a group rather than focusing on a single action. You will form a much clearer image of what the person is thinking and feeling by allowing yourself to take in all the information that is being presented. Here are twenty one of the main body language cues.

21 Essential Body Language Cues & Signals

1. **Body hunched** - low confidence
2. **Clenched fists** - aggression
3. **Crossed arms** - shut off, uncomfortable
4. **Dragging feet** - lethargy
5. **Dropped shoulders** - lethargy or boredom
6. **Fidgeting with objects, hands** - nervousness, guilt
7. **Hands behind head** - arrogance, superiority
8. **Hands on hips** - in defiance
9. **Hands on table** - in agreement
10. **Head down** - timidity
11. **Head rested on hand** - bored, disinterested
12. **Leaning away** - discomfort with the situation
13. **Leaning in closer** - interest, comfortable
14. **Looking at watch** - boredom
15. **Looking away to the left** – lying, using imagination
16. **Messaging temples** - anxiety
17. **Nodding** - interest, agreement or understanding
18. **Shaking of legs** - a sign of stress
19. **Shifty eyes** – nervousness, guilt
20. **Tapping foot** - impatient or nervous
21. **Wiping hands on clothes** - nervousness

Detecting Deception

The Face:

Our faces reveal multitudes about what we are thinking, feeling, intending. A slack jaw hints that we've been surprised, flared nostrils suggest hostility. Drooping eyelids indicate sadness or exhaustion. This is to say nothing of the powerful messages communicated by the face in the downward glance, the flirtatious "look away," or the piercing stare.

These well-known and instantly recognizable facial expressions are but a few of the literally thousands of expressions and movements that researchers have recorded and mapped over the years while observing the face. Because our facial expressions are reliable indicators of our true emotional state, they are a Mentalist's best friend. While not every lift of the eyebrows or tightening of the lips will yield an absolute "truth" or "lie" verdict, you can glean much from careful study of the face. Master the face and you'll soon discover a world of information about coworkers, clients, friends and strangers that was previously hiding in plain sight.

The facial expressions worth knowing about can be grouped into seven basic emotions: fear, happiness, sadness, anger, contempt, disgust and surprise. Through his groundbreaking research in the 1960s in the jungles of Papua New Guinea, Paul Ekman disproved earlier theories that human expressions were learned, and instead showed that our facial expressions are innate and universal. Genuine facial expressions are almost always symmetrical. From frowns to smiles, we typically reveal true feelings evenly on both sides of the face. Just like a picture hanging perfectly on a wall, one's face looks it's most natural when balanced. Six of the seven core emotions are displayed genuinely with symmetrical expressions on the face. What this means is that if someone shows signs of surprise on just one side of their face, chances are they already knew what you just told them.

Involuntary movements around the eyes distinguish a genuine smile from a fake one. Sincere smiles involve two main parts: upward-turned corners of the mouth, and narrowing of the eyelids to form "crow's feet" at the corners of the eyes. Humans can consciously and fairly easily manipulate the muscles around the mouth to form the bottom half of a smile, but it's nearly impossible for us to fake the muscle movements of the top half, the area around the eyes. So if your lover's smile doesn't engage the eyes or, if it flashes only on one side of the face, there might be trouble in paradise.

While true happiness is revealed by the eyes, true sadness is revealed in the muscles of the chin. Only one in ten people can pull down the corners of their lips without also moving their chin muscles. This extra chin movement is the artificial part of a frown, and thus the giveaway. If you see the chin muscles engage, chances are you're seeing an insincere display of sadness.

The largest myth about deception, that liars don't like to make eye contact, is false. The reality is a truth-teller is just as likely to break eye contact as someone who is lying. In fact, liars tend to exhibit more eye contact, and for longer stretches, because they believe this will help to "sell" their story.

When we are being truthful, our facial expressions are naturally expressed in synch with our physical gestures. With deception, as with comedy, timing is everything. Want to fake your rage by slamming your fists on the table? Better sync it just right with the angry expression on your face. Otherwise it will appear unnatural and deceptive. Genuine emotional displays are almost always simultaneous.

The Language

Here are 10 common ways that liars use words to obscure the truth.

Liars will repeat a question verbatim. Repeating a question in full is a common stalling tactic used by people looking for an extra moment to prepare their deceptive reply. In natural conversation, people will sometimes repeat part of a question, but restating the entire question is highly awkward and unnecessary, they clearly heard you the first time.

Liars will take a guarded tone. A suspicious or guarded approach isn't usually called for, and may indicate that they are concealing something, whether it's the truthful answer or their attitude toward you for asking the question in the first place.

Liars won't use contractions in their denials. Bill Clinton provides the classic example of what interrogators call a "non-contracted denial" when he said "I did not have sexual relations with that woman." The extra emphasis in the denial is unnecessary if someone is telling the truth. I didn't have sex with her is how the honest person is likely to phrase his claim of innocence.

Liars love euphemisms. It's human nature not to implicate ourselves in wrongdoing. This holds true even for liars, who will shy away from dwelling on their deception if possible. One way they do this is opting for softening their language; so, instead of saying "I didn't steal the purse" they may say "I didn't take the purse." If you ask someone a direct question about their involvement in an incident and they change your words to something softer, raise your deception alert.

Liars overemphasize their truthfulness. "To tell you the truth…" "Honestly…" "I swear to you…" When people use these bolstering statements to emphasize their honesty, there's a good chance they are hiding something. Learning to baseline someone's normal behavior is important in situations such as this: You want to listen for normal or harmless use of such phrases. There's no need to add them if you really are telling the truth, so be on guard.

Liars avoid or confuse pronouns. We use a fair amount of pronouns in normal conversation. They are a sign of comfortable speech, and they may disappear or be misused by someone who is trying to be extra careful with his words.

Liars hedge their statements. We hear them in court testimony, political hearings and TV confessional interviews all the time: qualifying statements that leave an out for the person on the hot seat. "As far as I recall…" "If you really think about it…" "What I remember is…" Hedged statements aren't an absolute indicator of deception, but an overuse of such qualifying phrases certainly should raise suspicion that a person isn't being totally up front with what he or she knows. With careful study of someone's language, you can ascertain an immense amount of information without ever having seen them.

Neuro Linguistic Programming

Neuro-Linguistic Programming (NLP) is an incredibly powerful, and often misunderstood and misused tool that enables people to manipulate the structures of human communication as to influence the mind. Developed by Richard Bandler and John Grinder, NLP explores the relationships between how we think (neuro), how we communicate (linguistic) and our patterns of behavior and emotion (programming).

While I personally do not agree with all the concepts and methods that fall under the NLP category, nor do I have faith in the effectiveness of certain techniques there are quite a few that are absolutely delightful, and deceptively useful.

I'm only going to share with you the core principals and techniques that I have found most useful in my work as a Mentalist, if you're so inclined feel free to search the internet and fill your head with all of the NLP jargon you can take. Trust me; there is plenty of it out there. Let's move on to the needful things…

Anchoring

Anchoring is reminiscent of Pavlov's experiments with dogs. Pavlov sounded a bell as the animal was given food. The animals heard the bell, and then salivated when they saw the food. After some repetitions of the bell and the food, the bell alone elicited salivation. This is anchoring in a nutshell. NLP offers us cunning ways to make use of this.

Anchors are stimuli that call forth states of mind, thoughts and emotions. For example, touching someone's shoulder with your hand could be an anchor. Some anchors are involuntary. So the smell of bread may take you back to your childhood. A song may remind you of a certain person. A touch can bring back memories and past states. These anchors work automatically and you may or may not be aware of the triggers.

Establishing an anchor means producing the stimuli (the anchor) when the desired state is experienced so that the desired state is joined to the anchor. For example touching the left shoulder of the person while they are in the desired state will join the touch to the state.

Activating or firing the anchor means producing the anchor after it has been conditioned so that the desired state occurs. For example, touching the left shoulder after the anchor has been established so that this action produces the desired state.

Anchors can be visual, auditory or kinesthetic. A visual anchor could be a wave of the hand or a certain colour that you have anchored to a desired state. Auditory anchors can be a clicking of the fingers, a word or phrase or a specific sound set to elicit the desired state. Kinesthetic anchors are generally touches. From a touch on the shoulder to a handshake, you can program people to elicit just about any response from any well set anchor.

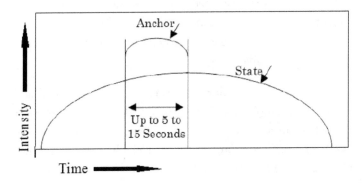

The above chart shows the relation from the time you establish the anchor and the intensity of the desired state your subject is in when you set the anchor. The chart will actually establish the ground rules for setting a successful anchor.

Your anchors should be short. Whether you are using a touch, a phrase or an image as your anchor, you should only elicit the anchor for five to fifteen seconds when initially setting the anchor.

The first step of setting an anchor is to get your subject into the desired state. You can do this by asking them to visualize a time when they felt this way, or showing them object that entice that response. Your subject must be able to access the desired state in order for you to anchor it.

Always set your anchors when your subject is ALMOST at peak state; see the chart above. By doing this you are CAPTURING not just the desired state, but the desired state IN a state of acceleration or peaking. When you later fire off your anchor, your subject will instantly be taken into the perpetual incline towards the desired state. This is a very powerful and extremely overlooked crux of the ultimate anchor. To really see incredible anchoring at work, take some time to search YouTube for the amazing English Mentalist, Derren Brown.

The NLP Eye Accessing Cues

Being able to notice the direction of a person's eye movements, and to recognize what they mean for that particular individual, provides information about how and what they are processing (or 'thinking' in the broadest sense of the term). Often the person themselves will not be aware of how they are thinking yet it is available for the sharp-eyed and skilled observer.

So, let's say you are explaining to a colleague how to do something and they say they do not understand, while looking UP to either the left or the right (indicating that they are visualizing or trying to visualize). This could indicate that they need you to demonstrate, rather than verbally explain, so they will be able to see how to do it.

What if you ask a friend a direct question and they look up and to the left, which denotes 'constructing images.' Let's just say you don't need to construct images to tell the truth... quite contrary.

Memorize the following chart, remember that this represent you facing the person forwards.

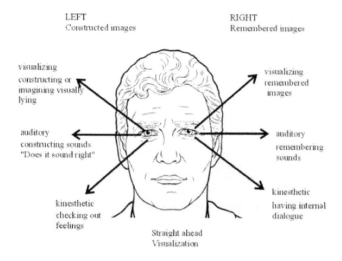

LEFT
Constructed images

RIGHT
Remembered images

visualizing
constructing or
imagining visually
lying

visualizing
remembered
images

auditory
constructing sounds
"Does it sound right"

auditory
remembering
sounds

kinesthetic
checking out
feelings

kinesthetic
having internal
dialogue

Straight ahead
Visualization

Upper Left, Visual Construction (VC): The person looking into that direction is constructing the image of a visual scene. The person's eye could go to this direction when he is asked about the color of his 'dream' car.

Upper Right, Visual Remembering (VR): The person looking into that direction is remembering the image of a visual scene. That's the direction someone could look at when he is asked about the color of his car.

Middle Left, Auditory Construction (AC): The person looking into that direction is constructing a sound. That's the direction the person's eye could go to when asked a question like, "what do you think Joe will tell you when you meet him tomorrow?"

Middle Right, Auditory Remembering (AR): The person looking into that direction is remembering a sound. That's the direction the person's eye could go to when asked a question like, "how did your manager's voice sound yesterday?"

Lower Left, Kinesthetic (K): This is the direction someone's eyes go to when they are accessing their feelings. That's the direction a person's eyes could go to when asked something like, "how did it feel to fail that exam?"

Lower Right, Auditory Digital (AD): This is the direction someone's eyes go to when they talk to themselves.

Below is the link to a wonderful online quizzing game that will test your knowledge and increase your speed!

www.nlp-practitioners.com/interactive/nlp-eye-access-cues-game.php

Conclusion

From 'Psychic Lies' to 'Mental Spies:' We have certainly covered an enormous amount of information for such a short book. I know it is has been at times a lot to digest but if you study the methods and techniques in this book and practice them daily, they will change the way you see the world, the way you see people and the way you walk into every situation. It is easy in the quest for knowledge to find yourself alone at the top, so always surround yourself with like-minded people who share your love for information.

"Beware of he who would deny you access to information, for in his heart he dreams himself your master."

-Sid Meier's Alpha Centauri

58

APPENDIX

A few invaluable worthwhile mentions on the web:

www.MXPublishing.com

The Skeptics Society & Skeptic Magazine

The Skeptic's Dictionary

Center for Nonverbal Studies

The Nonverbal Dictionary

www.TheWorldOfJoeRiggs.com

www.Sherlock-Holmes.org.uk

www.Sherlockology.com

www.BakerStreetBabes.com

www.BakerStreetBeat.com

www.Statistics.com

Also from MX Publishing

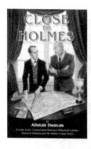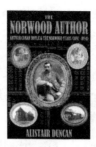

Four books on Sir Arthur Conan Doyle by Alistair Duncan including a an overview of all the stories (**Eliminate The Impossible**), a London guide (**Close to Holmes**), the winner of the Howlett Award 2011 (**The Norwood Author**) and the book on Undershaw (**An Entirely New Country**).

Short fiction collections from Tony Reynolds (**Lost Stories of Sherlock Holmes**), Gerard Kelly (**The Outstanding Mysteries of Sherlock Holmes**) and Bertram Fletcher Robinson (**Aside Arthur Conan Doyle**).

www.mxpublishing.com

Also From MX Publishing

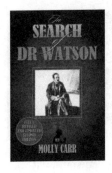  

A biography (**In Search of Dr Watson**), a travel guide (**Sherlock Holmes and Devon**), a novel where Sherlock Holmes battles The Phantom (**Rendezvous at The Populaire**), a novel featuring Dr.Watson (**Watson's Afghan Adventure**), a fantasy novel (**Shadowfall**) and an intriguing collection of papers from The Hound (**The Official Papers Into The Matter Known as The Hound of The Baskervilles**).

www.mxpublishing.com

Two 'Female Sherlock Holmes' novels (**The Sign of Fear** and **A Study In Crimson**) the definitive **A Chronology of Sir Arthur Conan Doyle**, a biography of **Bertram Fletcher Robinson**, reprint of the novel **Wheels of Anarchy** and the 4 'Lost Playlets of P.G.Wodehouse (**Bobbles and Plum**).

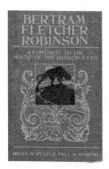

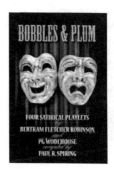

www.mxpublishing.com

Also From MX Publishing

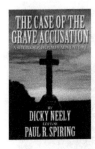

The Case of The Grave Accusation

The creator of Sherlock Holmes has been accused of murder. Only Holmes and Watson can stop the destruction of the Holmes legacy.

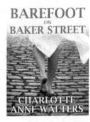

Barefoot on Baker Street

Epic novel of the life of a Victorian workhouse orphan featuring Sherlock Holmes and Moriarty.

Case of Witchcraft

A tale of witchcraft in the Northern Isles, in which long-concealed secrets are revealed -- including some that concern the Great Detective himself!

www.mxpublishing.com

Also From MX Publishing

The Affair In Transylvania

Holmes and Watson tackle Dracula in deepest Transylvania in this stunning adaptation by film director Gerry O'Hara

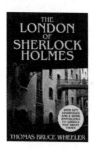

The London of Sherlock Holmes

400 locations including GPS co-ordinates that enable Google Street view of the locations around London in all the Homes stories

I Will Find The Answer

Sequel to Rendezvous At The Populaire, Holmes and Watson tackle Dr.Jekyll.

www.mxpublishing.com

Also From MX Publishing

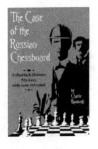

The Case of The Russian Chessboard

Short novel covering the dark world of Russian espionage sees Holmes and Watson on the world stage facing dark and complex enemies.

Shadowblood

Sequel to Shadowfall, Holmes and Watson tackle blood magic, the vilest form of sorcery.

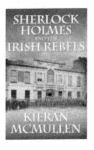

Sherlock Holmes and The Irish Rebels

It is early 1916 and the world is at war. Sherlock Holmes is well into his spy persona as Altamont.

Also from MX Publishing

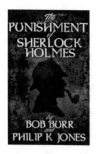

The Punishment of Sherlock Holmes

"deliberately and successfully funny"

The Sherlock Holmes Society of London

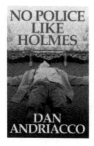

No Police Like Holmes

It's a Sherlock Holmes symposium, and murder is involved. The first case for Sebastian McCabe.

In The Night, In The Dark

Winner of the Dracula Society Award – a collection of supernatural ghost stories from the editor of the Sherlock Holmes Society of London journal.

Also from MX Publishing

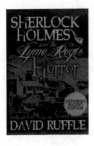

Sherlock Holmes and The Lyme Regis Horror

Fully updatad 2nd edition of this bestselling Holmes story set in Dorset.

My Dear Watson

Winner of the Suntory Mystery Award for fiction and translated from the original Japanese. Holmes greatest secret is revealed – Sherlock Holmes is a woman.

Mark of The Baskerville Hound

100 years on and a New York policeman faces a similar terror to the great detective.

Also From MX Publishing

Sherlock Holmes Whos Who

All the characters from the entire canon catalogued and profiled.

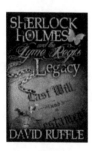

Sherlock Holmes and The Lyme Regis Legacy

Sequel to the Lyme Regis Horror and Holmes and Watson are once again embroiled in murder in Dorset.

Sherlock Holmes and The Discarded Cigarette

London 1895. A well known author, a theoretical invention made real and the perfect crime.

Also From MX Publishing

Sherlock Holmes and The Whitechapel Vampire

Jack The Ripper is a vampire, and Holmes refusal to believe it could lead to his downfall.

Tales From The Strangers Room

A collection of writings from more than 20 Sherlockians with author profits going to The Beacon Society.

The Secret Journal of Dr Watson

Holmes and Watson head to the newly formed Soviet Union to rescue the Romanovs.

www.mxpublishing.com

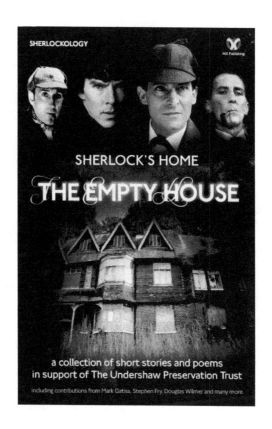

Sherlock's Home – The Empty House

With contributions from Stephen Fry, Mark Gatiss, Douglas Wilmer and more than 30 Sherlock Holmes writers this amazing book was put together to raise awareness for the www.saveundershaw.com campaign – aiming to save Sir Arthur Conan Doyle's home from destrutction.

CPSIA information can be obtained
at www.ICGtesting.com
Printed in the USA
BVHW041351251119
564766BV00010B/107/P

9 781780 922621